Building
Relationships
Within
God's Family

COMMUNITY

Interactions Small Group Series

Building
Relationships
Within
God's Family

COMMUNITY

BILL HYBELS

WITH KEVIN AND SHERRY HARNEY

■ ZONDERVAN®   WILLOW
                 Willow Creek Resources

ZONDERVAN.com/
AUTHORTRACKER
follow your favorite authors

ZONDERVAN®

Community
Copyright © 1998 by Willow Creek Association

Requests for information should be addressed to:

Zondervan, *Grand Rapids, Michigan 49530*

ISBN 978-0-310-26591-7

Interior design by Rick Devon and Michelle Espinoza

Printed in the United States of America

08 09 10 11 12 13 14 15 16 17 18 19 20 • 26 25 24 23 22 21 20 19 18 17 16 15 14 13 12 11 10 9 8

CONTENTS

Interactions

In 1992, Willow Creek Community Church, in partnership with Zondervan and the Willow Creek Association, released a curriculum for small groups entitled the Walking with God series. In just three years, almost a half million copies of these small group study guides were being used in churches around the world. The phenomenal response to this curriculum affirmed the need for relevant and biblical small group materials.

At the writing of this curriculum, there are nearly 3,000 small groups meeting regularly within the structure of Willow Creek Community Church. We believe this number will increase as we continue to place a central value on small groups. Many other churches throughout the world are growing in their commitment to small group ministries as well, so the need for resources is increasing.

In response to this great need, the Interactions small group series has been developed. Willow Creek Association and Zondervan have joined together to create a whole new approach to small group materials. These discussion guides are meant to challenge group members to a deeper level of sharing, create lines of accountability, move followers of Christ into action, and help group members become fully devoted followers of Christ.

Suggestions for Individual Study

1. Begin each session with prayer. Ask God to help you understand the passage and to apply it to your life.
2. A good modern translation, such as the New International Version, the New American Standard Bible, or the New Revised Standard Version will give you the most help. Questions in this guide are based on the New International Version.
3. Read and reread the passage(s). You must know what the passage says before you can understand what it means and how it applies to you.
4. Write your answers in the spaces provided in the study guide. This will help you to express clearly your understanding of the passage.
5. Keep a Bible dictionary handy. Use it to look up unfamiliar words, names, or places.

SUGGESTIONS FOR GROUP STUDY

1. Come to the session prepared. Careful preparation will greatly enrich your time in group discussion.
2. Be willing to join in the discussion. The leader of the group will not be lecturing, but will encourage people to discuss what they have learned in the passage. Plan to share what God has taught you in your individual study.
3. Stick to the passage being studied. Base your answers on the verses being discussed rather than on outside authorities such as commentaries or your favorite author or speaker.
4. Try to be sensitive to the other members of the group. Listen attentively when they speak, and be affirming whenever you can. This will encourage more hesitant members of the group to participate.
5. Be careful not to dominate the discussion. By all means participate! But allow others to have equal time.
6. If you are the discussion leader, you will find additional suggestions and helpful ideas in the leader's notes.

ADDITIONAL RESOURCES AND TEACHING MATERIALS

At the end of this study guide you will find a collection of resources and teaching materials to help you in your growth as a follower of Christ. You will also find resources that will help your church develop and build fully devoted followers of Christ.

Introduction: Building Relationships Within God's Family

I gathered with a group of friends to give a farewell party to the summer of '95. There was a wide assortment of people around the dinner table that night, with a spiritual range that spanned the entire continuum from pre-seekers to mature Christians.

When I noticed there was just surface conversation going on around the table, I said, "Would you all mind responding to one question?" I continued, "Would you be willing to describe the *most memorable moment* in your life from the summer of '95?"

The first to respond was a man who was sitting just to my right. Next to him was a young woman. He said quite romantically, "The most memorable moment of my summer was when I first met eyes with the beautiful woman sitting next to me." Then he gave the exact time and date they met and said, "It may turn out to be the most memorable moment of my *life*." Some around the table started to blush, and others started to gag.

Next there was a young woman who said, "I'll tell you my most memorable moment. It was my birthday this summer." She described how her boyfriend, who was also at the table, sent her flowers, wrote her a note, and took her out for a romantic dinner and a late-night walk on the beach.

The next guy described a great sailing trip he had taken with a friend. The sailing conditions were perfect, and the trip was unforgettable. "But," he said, "the best part of all was the deep conversations we had." This was the highlight of his summer.

One man in the circle was a chef, and he told us about the time he prepared a gourmet dinner for three couples who are his very close friends. He had worked days preparing for this dinner and when the evening came they sat around the table for hours enjoying wonderful food and conversation. He said, "It was the kind of conversation you think about for weeks afterward." He told us it gave him incredible pleasure to provide the opportunity for all that to happen.

On and on it went. At some point in the discussion I recognized a common thread developing. There wasn't a single mention of the material world in the conversations of summer high- lights. No one said, "My *best* memory of the summer of '95 was when I bought a house," car, or a boat, or some toy. There was no mention of achievements, promotions at work, first-place trophies, or sales awards. Every significant moment mentioned around the table that night centered on relation- ships. Despite the wide variety of people at the table, and despite their spiritual ranges, it was their relationships that brought the greatest amount of joy in their lives.

Like the group I gathered with at the end of the summer of '95, we all hunger for meaningful relationships. We value friendships and people above almost everything else. We all have a deep need to build genuine community in our lives. In this series of interactions we will grow in our ability to build healthy relationships and learn to develop and nurture lasting community. After discovering the heartbeat of community, we will learn about the cost of building lasting relationships in God's family. We will also identify what it takes to move beyond superficial relationships. Then we will identify some of the relational viruses we face, as well as the value of estab- lishing clear boundaries as we build lasting friendships in God's family. Finally, we will learn how to extend the gift of community to those who have not yet learned how much they matter to God.

THE HEARTBEAT OF COMMUNITY

Taking of the mask "Be Real"

THE BIG PICTURE

Chicago Tribune writer Marla Paul took a risk when she wrote a self-revealing column confessing her sadness and frustration over her own inability to build and sustain friendships. She wrote this column expecting little, if any, response. However, she was inundated with letters from others experiencing the same kind of isolation and frustration.

One person wrote, "I've often felt that I'm standing outside looking through the window of a party to which I was not invited." What a vivid picture! Do you ever feel that way? Do you ever have a sense of being on the outside looking in?

Another woman wrote, "I have this fear of becoming a very lonely, old widow sitting around and listening to the clock tick." This fear, she says, just about paralyzes her life. It is probably a well-founded fear, because she confessed in her letter that she has no sense of community. She has no family. She has no friendship or small group or church community of which she's a part. She feels that she's going to die alone, and she may be right.

In the summer of '95, many people died in Chicago's heat wave. I was shocked to read that forty-one of them were buried in a mass grave called "The Potter's Field." Not a single person surfaced to claim their bodies or grieve their passing. Forty-one people died alone.

Marla Paul ended her column about loneliness with these words: "Sometimes it seems easier to just give up and accept disconnectedness as a dark and unshakable companion; but,

that's not the companion I want." She writes, "So I will perse-
vere." She is going to keep longing, searching, trying, and
hoping that someday she will be able to discover and develop
community.

A WIDE ANGLE VIEW

1   Describe a time in your life when you experienced real
community and connectedness with other people.

Where do you experience community now?

A BIBLICAL PORTRAIT

Read Genesis 2:15–25

2   What do you learn about loneliness and the human
need for community from this passage?

*a need to Relate to someone
of your own origin. Reproduction*

Read Snapshot "Knowing and Being Known"

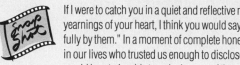

KNOWING AND BEING KNOWN

If I were to catch you in a quiet and reflective mood, and if you were aware enough of the longings and yearnings of your heart, I think you would say, "I would love to know others deeply and be known fully by them." In a moment of complete honesty, I think we would all love it if there were some people in our lives who trusted us enough to disclose the deep and tender parts of themselves. I think we would love to be able to unlock some of the vaulted feelings we carry to people who really cared. Most of us gravitate toward friendships, dating, marriage, golf leagues, racquetball clubs, or small groups because somewhere floating around within us is a yearning to know and be known by others.

3

What are some of the things that keep us from opening our hearts and lives on a deep level so we can be known by others?

TRust , shame , Fear,

4

Suppose you made this commitment: "I am going to open my life in a way that allows others to know me deeply. I am going to find some people I will allow to see my deepest joys, needs, struggles, and victories. I am also going to invite them to open their hearts and lives to me on this same deep level."

What are some of the possible risks you would be taking?

exposing personal matters / Issues

What are some of the possible joys you might experience?

Healing, freedom

Read Snapshot "Loving and Being Loved"

LOVING AND BEING LOVED

Another component in community is loving and being loved. Unless you are exchanging deeply committed levels of love with a few people, you will die slowly on the inside. This is precisely why so many people feel almost nothing at all. Through the whole course of their lives, they have never exchanged deep levels of love with anybody. It hasn't happened with their parents. It hasn't happened with a spouse. And sadly, it hasn't happened with friends. By this point in life they have become completely numb to the possibility that they might experience a passionate, loving relationship. This is not God's plan for us. He hungers for us to be loved and to give love to others. As a matter of fact, He wants this for us even more than we hunger for it ourselves.

5

Who in your life has poured out consistent and deep levels of love on you, and how have they expressed this love?

My mom
encouragement, words of wisdom
nuturing, providing, teaching
Praying for me, introduced me
to God

6

Finish the statements below:

- I experience love the most from others when they . . .

Speak & smile
show Respect

- I am most comfortable expressing love by . . .

Helping others
Saying it with words
and deeds

- I find it hard to receive love from others because . . .

I haven't Recieved a lot

Read Snapshot "Serving and Being Served"

SERVING AND BEING SERVED

Community is also about serving and being served. The single most stirring example of this is recorded in John 13. In this chapter Jesus takes the position of the lowest servant and washes the feet of His followers. He gives them a powerful example and then calls them to follow. Servanthood is at the very core of community. To sustain deep relationships over a long period of time, there must be humility and a willingness to serve each other. There also must be a willingness to be served. When Jesus took a towel and a bowl of water and washed the feet of His followers, He established once and for all the absolute centrality of serving for all who desire to live in community.

7 How have you been served by others and how has their Christlike service helped to build community?

8 With whom would you want to move toward a deeper level of community? What act of service will you render to help develop a deeper relationship and sense of community?

Read Snapshot "Celebrating and Being Celebrated"

CELEBRATING AND BEING CELEBRATED

If you haven't had a good blush recently, read a short book in the Bible called Song of Songs. It's a record of a bride and a bridegroom writing poetic and romantic notes to each other. They are freely celebrating every conceivable aspect of each other's personalities, character, and physical characteristics. At one point the groom says, "You have made my heart beat fast with a single glance from your eyes. How beautiful is your love, my bride. How much better it is than the finest of wines." Near the end of the book they both agree that a loving community in the context of a marriage is just about as good as it gets. They refer to the wealth and fortunes of a hugely successful man they know, and they say to each other, "We wouldn't think of trading what we have for all of his riches. We have community."

This couple enhanced their community and the quality of their relationship by creatively celebrating each other. They did what many of us fail to do. They noticed each other. They observed each other carefully. Then they decided to highlight what they found attractive and desirable and praiseworthy about each other and took the time to express it. We have the ability to delight each other's hearts when we celebrate one another.

9 Take time as a group to celebrate each other. Have each member of your group ask one or two other members to finish this statement: If you were suddenly taken out of my life, I would miss your_____.

PUTTING YOURSELF IN THE PICTURE

AN EXPRESSION OF THANKS

If there is a person in your life who has freely poured out deep levels of love on you, take time in the coming weeks to express your thankfulness. Call them on the phone, write them a note, or take them out to lunch. Communicate how much their love means to you and how much you appreciate the community you have together. Take time to celebrate what they have meant and continue to mean in your life.

A COMMITMENT TO CELEBRATION

Make a list of three people who are not in your small group but who you want to celebrate and affirm. Use the same format as you used in question nine to let them know what you would miss about them if you were no longer in community. Tell them why you appreciate being in community with them.

COUNTING THE COST OF COMMUNITY

REFLECTIONS FROM SESSION 1

1. If you took time in this past week to thank a person who has loved you deeply over the years, tell your group how that person responded.
2. If you took time since your last small group to tell a friend how much you would miss them if they were no longer in your life, how did your friend respond to your words? What kind of conversation grew out of your vulnerable sharing?

THE BIG PICTURE

There's a great story that dates back to the early sixties when Vince Lombardi took over the reins of the Green Bay Packers. The Packer franchise was struggling—the team had been losing for almost ten straight years. They were on the bottom of the league standings, and team morale was sagging.

Into this dismal situation comes Vince Lombardi, the new coach. He had been given the challenge of turning the franchise around. He was all pumped up and excited about turning the team around, so he began meeting with the team, leading practices, training, motivating, and doing all he could to inspire his players. At one point during a practice he got so frustrated with the players that he blew his whistle and said, "Everybody stop and gather round." He said, "This isn't working. Either I'm not training you right or you're not getting it. In either case, what we're doing is not working." Then he knelt down, picked up the pigskin, and said, "Let's start at the beginning. *This* is a football."

One guy said, "Slow down, Coach, you're losing me." But Lombardi persisted with his course of action, saying, "This is a football, and these are yard markers, and that's the goal post, and I'm the coach, and you're the players." He went on in the most elementary of ways to explain the *basics* of football. History tells us that from that point in time the whole direction of the Green Bay Packers turned around.

This story has found its way into the folklore of the Green Bay Packers and professional football. It's used in different settings because everybody knows that every once in a while we all need to get back to the basics.

A WIDE ANGLE VIEW

1 Take a moment on your own to think about how you would define each of the following terms. Try to be as basic and clear as possible.

- Friendship

> ✓Trust worthy
> encouragement
> Pat'ence

- Relationship

> have something in common

anything
defined by people

> No good
> discpline
> common ground

- Community

A BIBLICAL PORTRAIT

Read Philippians 2:1–11

2 When you think about being in relationship and community with others, what does it mean to:

- Be like-minded

- working toward the same purpose
- methods may be different, message is
* the same*
- Christ centered

- Have the same love

The focus is to please Christ and to
at best imitate Christ. Patience, Kindness

- Be one in spirit and purpose

- Humbly consider others better than yourself

Why are all of these critical for deep and lasting community?

3 In verses 5–8 we read of the attitude and actions of Jesus. How is Jesus' life an example of counting the cost of community?

What do you learn from the example of Jesus that will help you develop deeper relationships?

SHARPENING THE FOCUS

Read Snapshot "Friendship Is Not"

FRIENDSHIP IS NOT

If we are going to count the cost of community, we must first be honest about our own natural selfishness when it comes to relationships. As we look for friends, we often think about what we can gain from the relationship. Let me try to clarify a few things friendship is *not*. Friendship is not about finding someone to take care of us and meet our needs. It is not about hitching our lives to a rising star for self-advancement. And it is certainly not pretending we care about someone so they will join our cause or buy our product. The bottom line of friendship was discussed in our last session: it is about knowing and being known, loving and being loved, serving and being served, and celebrating and being celebrated.

---

4 What are some of the possible consequences and problems a person might face if they enter a friendship with the following attitudes:

- I'm looking for a friend who is just like me. We need to see things eye to eye.

- I want a friend who will make me feel better about myself when I'm with them.

- I want a friend who is ready and willing to meet my needs and care for me.

5 Respond to this statement: *Building a strong friendship involves blood, sweat, and tears. My closest friends are people who have walked with me through the good times and the bad times.*

Read Snapshot "Friendships Take Work"

FRIENDSHIPS TAKE WORK

If we are going to move from aloneness toward community, we must face the sobering reality that building friendships can be a lengthy and challenging endeavor. It's a process that requires energy, risk, and quite possibly, hurt. When the Bible says real friendships are like silver and gold, it is underscoring their incredible value and worth. The Bible also uses the metaphor of digging for gold when referring to friendships because both involve hard work and commitment over time.

6 Picture a relationship you treasure. What makes it so valuable to you?

Read Snapshot "Friendships Take Time"

FRIENDSHIPS TAKE TIME

Some time ago we added a staff member at our church who had moved from another part of the country. As some of us were welcoming him, we asked him how we could support him in prayer. He said, "One of the things I really need is to find some true friends."

A little later I said to him, "This is a great place to build friendships, but I have to tell you something. It might take a little longer than you expect." He said, "How long is long?"

I said, "My guess is it's going to take at least two years." Some time later he said to me, "I almost gagged when you said it might take two years to establish strong relationships. I wanted it to take two months."

7

Why does it usually take a long period of time to build a strong and lasting relationship?

8

Tell the group about some of the relationships you are investing yourself in at this time in your life. What can they do to encourage you in your commitment to build strong and lasting relationships?

PUTTING YOURSELF IN THE PICTURE

AN INVESTMENT OF TIME

Take time in the coming week to identify a friendship you value but have not invested much time in recently. Contact this person and invite them out for coffee or lunch. Let them know how much you value their friendship and that you desire to spend time with them.

CHECKING MOTIVES

Sometimes we develop friendships for the wrong reasons. Unless we slow down and examine our motives, it can be hard to identify when this is happening. Use the questions below for personal reflection as you check the motives and driving forces behind some of your relationships.

After identifying a specific friendship you are developing, reflect on the following questions:

- What originally attracted me to this person?
- What do I gain from being in this relationship?
- What do I give to this relationship and add to the other person's life?
- Do I actively seek ways to serve this person and build them up?

MOVING BEYOND SUPERFICIALITY

REFLECTIONS FROM SESSION 2

1. If you invested some time in a relationship you had been recently neglecting, what impact has this investment had on the relationship? If you meant to spend some time with a person you have not contacted recently, when will you do it? Who will keep you accountable?

2. If you took time to examine the motives behind your friendships, what did you learn about yourself? How can your small group pray for you as you seek to develop your relationships with pure motives?

THE BIG PICTURE

I took a relational risk one day as a senior in college. Little did I know then that my willingness to go out on a limb and intentionally move to a deeper level of relationship would change the course of my life. One of my professors at Trinity College was Dr. Gilbert Bilezikian. His love for God and concern for people moved my heart and made me want to get to know him better. But, to be honest, in my four years of college I don't think I had ever voluntarily walked up and introduced myself to any of my professors.

I remember thinking, "Wouldn't it be great if Dr. B. would be my friend?" But I also thought, "He's probably got all kinds of friends and doesn't need any more." One day I stayed after class and stood off to the side for a little while. Then I walked up to him very tentatively and said, "Dr. B., when you talk about the church in your lectures, my heart beats so fast I think it's going to come flying out of my chest. I wonder if we could talk about it in private some day." That was one of the biggest relational risks I've ever taken.

To my amazement, he said, "Let's do it right now." We went and sat down over a cup of coffee and started talking about life, faith, the church, and all sorts of other topics. We met for coffee and discussion again and again over the coming months and years. We became friends, and it was his influence on my life that gave birth to Willow Creek Community Church.

Sometimes I wonder, *What if I hadn't taken that step? What if I hadn't risked a little bit? What if I hadn't pushed beyond the safe level of relationship into a deeper level of friendship?*

You too may be one relationship away from a whole new chapter in the story of your life. You could be one friendship away from some new understanding, experience, or life dynamic. It's just a risk away.

A WIDE ANGLE VIEW

1   Tell your group about a time you took a risk and pushed beyond a superficial relationship into a deeper level of friendship.

How might your life be different today if you had not taken this risk?

A BIBLICAL PORTRAIT

Read John 4:4–26

2

What does the Samaritan woman say to move beyond superficial conversation to a deeper level of communication and relationship?

What does Jesus say to move the relationship from superficial conversation to a deeper level of communication?

SHARPENING THE FOCUS

Read Snapshot "Moving Beyond Superficiality"

MOVING BEYOND SUPERFICIALITY

One challenge we all face in the quest for community is to move beyond the level of superficiality. When we first start forming friendships, conversations tend to be a bit shallow. That's okay. Trust has to be built and the knowledge base must develop. But if relationships stay stuck at the surface level, we will find our hearts crying out, "I was created for more than this. I need to go deeper." At this point we need to press beyond the wall of superficiality to deep conversation, communication, and sharing

3

What keeps us relating on a superficial level and hinders us from going deeper in relationship with others?

4

What has helped you take risks and push beyond the wall of superficiality to a deeper level of friendship and community?

Read Snapshot "The Value of a Good Question"

THE VALUE OF A GOOD QUESTION

The single best tool I've discovered to move relationships beyond superficiality is the asking of a carefully thought-out question. This question must be accompanied by an invitation for an honest and sincere answer. If we stay with safe surface questions, our relationships will remain shallow. If we move deeper with questions and conversations that break the superficiality barrier, we will watch our relationships move to deeper and deeper levels. Here are a few of my favorite questions:

- *How are you doing, really?* How are things at home, really? How is work, really? That one word, "really," makes all the difference in the world.

- *How do you feel about that?* When someone tells you about something that has happened in their life, follow it up with this question.

- *What are you thinking about right now?* This is a question you can ask a friend, a child, or anyone you spend time with. Give them an open door to tell you what's on their mind.

5

Break into pairs and take about five minutes to ask each other one of the above questions. After asking, take time to really listen.

As a group, describe what you learned about each other.

Read Snapshot "The Place of Community with God"

THE PLACE OF COMMUNITY WITH GOD

Your ability to experience and enjoy the fullness of human community is directly linked to your community with God. Many people wish they were doing better in their human relational world, but they don't see that there is a definite connection between their communion with God and the quality of their human relationships. Your relationship-building potential with your horizontal relationships is directly tied to the maturity level of your vertical relationship with God.

When you open up your heart to the love of God by trusting in Jesus Christ, His love fills you. It becomes the bedrock foundation out of which you move into human relationships. Your relationship with God, if it's mature and growing, gives you the inner security to take risks in human relationships. From that rich point of security and peace, you can move more freely in and around your relational world. You take pressure off the people around you because your source of security and strength is God, not them. I find that when my relationship with God is rich and growing, I move into human relationships with less fear. I am also more able to let human relationships go when their season comes to an end. And I can walk away from damaging relationships without feeling like I'm walking off into some dark abyss. I'm secure in my human relationships because my final security is in my relationship with God.

6 What barriers stand in the way of your developing a deeper relationship with God?

Bussiness, Honesty, commitment (time), ourselves (Flesh)

7 If you feel your relationship with God is intimate and strong at this time, how is this impacting your relationships with others?

If you have to honestly admit that your relationship with God is not very intimate at this time, what impact is this having on your relationships with others?

8 What specific goals do you need to set to move yourself toward deeper community and relationship with God? How can your small group members pray for you and keep you accountable as you grow deeper in your relationship with God?

PUTTING YOURSELF IN THE PICTURE

ASKING QUESTIONS

In the coming weeks, commit yourself to going deeper in conversations. Practice using barrier-breaking questions you learned about in this session. If your group members had other good questions for breaking the superficiality barrier, use them as well. You may even want to write down these questions on a card or piece of paper and keep it in your wallet or purse. The more you use these questions, the more natural they will become and the more you will see your conversations moving to a deeper level of communication.

MAKING SPACE FOR GOD

If you long for deeper human relationships, you need to also seek to grow in your relationship with God. This involves making space in your life to worship God and to be in His presence. Sit down with your schedule for the coming weeks and write down when you will spend time reading the Bible, praying, journaling, or whatever you do to grow in your relationship with the Father. Put God in your schedule as a first priority and be sure not to break your date.

HEALING RELATIONAL VIRUSES

REFLECTIONS FROM SESSION 3

1. How did you seek to go deeper in your conversations since your group last met? Were people responsive and open to going deeper? If so, in what ways?
2. If you have been intentionally making space for God in your life, how has this impacted your faith and your relationships with others?

THE BIG PICTURE

If you don't know who Fred McMurray was, then you probably were not born in the baby boom generation. Those of us who grew up in the middle of that bell-shaped baby boom curve remember him as the quintessential father in the show, "My Three Sons." Fred led that idyllic family of five in a cozy home on a tree-lined street in suburbia. It seemed every problem in that family was solved in twenty-six minutes. What a dad! Fred McMurray's three boys walked into adulthood as whole, healthy adults without a care in the world.

Thirty years later we don't see many all-American families on television anymore. Instead of "My Three Sons," we have shows like "My Two Dads." These days few homes are sending young people into adulthood whole and healthy, without a care in the world. Although you can still walk down tree-lined suburban streets and see lovely homes, what's going on inside those homes is often very different from what was happening thirty years ago.

It's highly unlikely that you'll find many breadwinning, family-oriented dads snuggled up next to their homemaking, family-oriented moms. More than likely you'll find two career-oriented parents who are stressed out. Their marriage isn't working all that well, and they're not very close to their kids. You might find a single-parent scenario that has challenges all its own. There's also a high probability there could be some substance abuse going on and financial pressures undermining the sense of security of the home. There is even the distinct possibility of verbal, emotional, physical, or sexual abuse.

Things have changed. Fewer and fewer sons and daughters these days are heading into adulthood hitting on all eight cylinders. On the contrary, record numbers of people are leaving their home environments with curious behavior patterns that were acquired to desperately cope with the chaos they encountered in their homes while growing up.

A WIDE ANGLE VIEW

1 What changes have you seen in the past three decades in the following areas:

- The attitudes and lifestyles of teenagers

- The focus and message of the media (TV, movies, books, and music)

- The role parents play in raising their children

- People's attitudes toward deep, committed relationships

A BIBLICAL PORTRAIT

Read Romans 12:9–13

2 Describe the difference between a "sincere love" and an "insincere love" in one of the following relationships. What does sincere love look like and what does insincere love look like?

- A friendship

- A marriage

- A professional relationship

- A parenting relationship

3 Choose one of the following challenges given by the apostle Paul and describe how it will help you build strong, healthy relationships.

"Hate what is evil, cling to what is good."
"Be devoted to one another in brotherly (sisterly) love."
"Honor one another above yourselves."
"Keep your spiritual fervor, serving the Lord."
"Be joyful in hope."
"Be patient in affliction."
"Be faithful in prayer."
"Practice hospitality."

SHARPENING THE FOCUS

Read Snapshot "Meeting the Smiths"

MEETING THE SMITHS

The Smiths lived on the corner of Elm and Vine. Without the neighbors ever knowing it, there was trouble behind the Smiths' white, picket fence. John Smith, the dad, was an emotionally distant father. He worked too hard and drank a little too much. Sally Smith, the mom, was a controller whose perfectionism drove everybody up the wall. John and Sally bore and raised four kids over a twenty-five year period. Each child developed his or her own way of coping with the hurt in their home. Along the way, each of them picked up some relational "viruses."

Suzie, the oldest daughter, learned how to be a pleaser. She knocked herself out doing everything she could to avoid setting off her father's temper and to meet the demanding expectations of a perfectionist mom. Suzie entered adulthood totally unaware of her own identity, her own feelings, her own preferences. Her goal was simple: Make everybody happy no matter the cost.

Jim, the second child, was so frightened by his father and overwhelmed by his domineering mother that he simply gave up early in the game and turned inward. Jim was a stuffer. He learned at an early age to push his feelings down. He didn't say much around the house and didn't get into much trouble. But you always got the impression there was a lot more going on underneath his calm exterior.

Sandy, the third child, became an achiever. She discovered that her dad would smile proudly when she came home with A's on her report card. Even her perfectionistic mother would manage a compliment if she could score higher than anyone else in her class on a particular test. Sandy launched into adulthood driven like a wild stallion. Her goal was to be the best at whatever she did.

John Jr. was the youngest. He became a rebel. He learned to evoke a dramatic response from his parents by doing wrong things. If he really messed up, his parents would actually talk to him. They'd interact with him, take him off to a side room, and try to figure out why he was acting up. He headed into adulthood with a chip on his shoulder and a tattoo on his forearm that read "Born to be wild."

From the outside, this family looked perfect. But inside, there was pain, tension, and hurt. It was a home filled with relational viruses. The fact is, most of us have developed relational patterns and viruses that are unhealthy. Like the Smiths, we need to identify our viruses and start dealing with them.

---

4 Describe some of the relational viruses that were spread in your home as you were growing up.

What impact are these viruses having on your life and relationships at this time?

5 How have you seen yourself experience healing in relationships and freedom from some of the relational viruses to which you have been exposed?

What specific actions and steps have helped you in the healing process?

6 Is there a relationship in your life at this time that needs healing?

How would you describe the problem or virus in this relationship?

How can your small group members pray for you and support you in this healing process?

Read Snapshot "Examining Your Relational Health"

EXAMINING YOUR RELATIONAL HEALTH

Until each of us is ready to recognize our own viruses and learn how they're distorting our own relationships, we're going to experience a nonstop series of relational frustrations. Some of you are tired of the fact that your marriage doesn't work, your relationship with your kids is strained, things at work don't go well. Everywhere you turn there's friction and dissatisfaction in your relational world. It may be that a relational virus continues to infect your life and relationships. If this is the case, it is time to have the courage to honestly examine your life and see where you need healing from.

---

7 Take some time for personal reflection and self-examination. Walk through your life and identify relationships that have broken up or have been filled with problems and tensions. Look for patterns of behavior on your part and see if you can identify any viruses. Use the space below as you reflect:

Name of the person with whom you had relational conflict	Source of the relational problem (virus)	The time in your life this occurred
_____	_____	_____
_____	_____	_____
_____	_____	_____
_____	_____	_____

8 Tell your group members about any patterns you found in your relational conflicts. What viruses did you identify?

What can you do to restore some of the brokenness in your relationships from the past?

What can your group members do to help you find healing in this area?

PUTTING YOURSELF IN THE PICTURE

PLAYING RELATIONAL HARDBALL

There may be many people who are happy to play in the relational minor leagues. But for those who want to play big-league relational ball, here's a challenge for you: Invite someone you know well and trust for lunch or dinner. Say to them, "I'd like to know if you see any viruses that I bring to this relationship. I'd like to know if you see any way that I distort our relationship. Do you sense anything in me that makes it difficult for our relationship to grow?" That's big-league relational play.

KNOWING GOD'S PLAN

God longs for us to have healthy and strong relationships. Romans 12:9–13 has a number of clear words of encouragement for those who desire to develop loving community. Take time in the coming week to memorize this short but powerful passage from the Bible.

SETTING HEALTHY RELATIONAL BOUNDARIES

REFLECTIONS FROM SESSION 4

1. If you decided to play relational hardball and asked a trusted friend to help you identify any relational viruses you might have in your life, what did you learn about yourself from this process?

2. If you memorized Romans 12:9–13, would you be willing to quote some or all of it for your group members? What impact have the challenges from this passage had on the way you relate to others?

THE BIG PICTURE

What do you do when you find yourself in a family with a person who has a severe relational virus? How do you manage your professional life if you work for, or with, someone who has a serious relational virus? How do you handle your church life when you run into people with relational viruses every single Sunday? How do you respond to the person in your neighborhood who has deep relational problems and who comes straight at you like a guided missile every time you walk out your front door? We live in a world filled with people who have relational viruses. What can we do to remain healthy and balanced in how we respond to these people?

This world is also filled with people who live with unresolved anger. Homes, neighborhoods, workplaces, and churches can all be anger-filled places where harsh words and actions can be hurled in your direction on a regular basis. How do you handle that? How do you establish healthy boundaries for these anger-filled relationships?

What if there's a controlling parent, boss, spiritual leader, or friend in your life? What if they seek to control you in ways that make you feel uncomfortable? How do you fend off their desire to run your life? What do you do with these controlling people?

How do you respond to people in your life who are constantly asking you to fix things for them or help them? We all know people who seek us for counsel over and over again but they never seem to get better. They want our time, our listening ear, our shoulder to cry on. And they want us to be available at the very moment of their need and crisis. The problem is, that they demand our time when others also need it. How do you respond to these people?

Giving & Recieving

How do you deal with the "Cousin Eddie" in your life who has asked you for financial help five times, and every time he's blown the money? Now he's at your door with tears in his eyes asking for help "Just this one last time!" He's saying, "You're a Christian. You're suppose to care. It's your responsibility to help me!" How do you deal with these situations in your life? How do you draw healthy boundaries in these kinds of relationships?

A WIDE ANGLE VIEW

1 How do you tend to respond when people in your life are needy and demanding of you?

How do you usually respond to those who unload their anger on you?

2

Tell about a time you said no to someone who came to you with an expressed need. How did it make you feel?

Think of a time you wanted to say no, but ended up saying yes to someone who came to you with a need. What kept you from saying no?

A BIBLICAL PORTRAIT

Read Exodus 18:13–27

3

Moses needed someone to come to him and say, "It's time to draw some clear boundaries. If you keep trying to meet everyone's needs, you're going to burn out!" How would you summarize the advice of Moses' father-in-law, Jethro?

In what way might the wisdom of this advice speak to you today?

SHARPENING THE FOCUS

Read Snapshot "Living Without Boundaries"

LIVING WITHOUT BOUNDARIES

People without relational boundaries are exposed and vulnerable to whatever relational virus comes their way. If they are relating to a powerful person, they can easily be manipulated or abused. When they are confronted by a needy person who says, "Help, help, help!" they are powerless to say no. They are prime targets for people who like to heap guilt on others. Every time "Cousin Eddie" comes over looking for a handout, they reach into their wallet or purse with no sense of discernment and with no clear boundaries.

If you live without relational boundaries long enough, one of two things usually happens. First, you begin to shrivel up and die inside. You have a hard time identifying your feelings and preferences because you spend all your time playing doctor to those people in your life with relational viruses. If you do this long enough, you can lose your personality all together. The second result of living without relational boundaries is that you become a bitter, anger-filled person. You keep a veneer of civility and concern for others, but you are resentful of being used by so many people. Neither option is a healthy one.

---

4 What are some of the consequences you have experienced when you have lived without relational boundaries?

5 If the consequences are painful, why do so many people continue to live without relational boundaries?

Read Snapshot "Unhealthy Walls"

UNHEALTHY WALLS

 Some people finally say, "I'm done living without relational boundaries. That's it! I'm going to do the opposite. I'm going to be sure I never get used or dumped on again!" They begin to erect a wall of refuge around them, brick by brick. They are committed to never getting hurt in a relationship again. Their wall of apathy and distance will protect them.

An angry person can come and start spewing out venom, but they don't care anymore because their wall protects them. Harsh words and attitudes bounce right off them. Cold, judgmental looks just don't affect their heart because it's as thick and hard as a brick wall. When "Cousin Eddie" comes over asking for a handout, they slam the door in his face. They're not going to get hurt by anybody. Of course, they are never going to have rich or meaningful relationships either. In their effort to avoid hurt they have also removed any chance of a rich relationship.

---

6. If you have ever tried to get close to a person who built a wall around their heart, tell your group about your experience.

What would you say to people who seek to protect themselves from relational hurt by erecting a stone wall around their hearts?

7. If you feel there is a wall around your heart today, what has caused you to build it, and what will be your first step in tearing it down?

Read Snapshot *"Flexible Boundaries"*

FLEXIBLE BOUNDARIES

 If the "no boundary" approach doesn't serve you well, and if a wall around your heart is not the answer, is there a middle ground? There is. We need to learn to create flexible boundaries that function much like an invisible force field. These boundaries can be activated to provide protection at times of need and deactivated when they are not needed.

How do flexible boundaries work? Imagine you're relating to a person who has a temper, but at this time they're not angry. You need to deactivate the force field and relate freely and lovingly with that person. But when something trips their button and they begin raging, erect your boundary. Activate your force field. Say to yourself, "This person is about ready to wound me deeply, and I'm not going to let that happen. They can rant and rave to any extent they want on their side of the fence, but not on my side. I know I matter to God, and I won't let them abuse me." You might need to remove yourself from the situation until they cool off. You might even need to lovingly tell them that you won't let them use you as the outlet for their anger. The key is, once they have cooled off, you need to be willing to let down the force field and open your life to them once again. Learning when to put up the force field and when to let it down takes time and wisdom.

8

Describe a relationship where you know a virus exists. Tell your group about times in this relationship when you need to activate a barrier and times when you can keep the barrier down.

How will you know the best time to activate your invisible force field to stop allowing this person to hurt you?

What specific attitudes or actions will show that you are not going to let the other person infect you with their relational virus?

PUTTING YOURSELF IN THE PICTURE

TEARING DOWN WALLS

Take time before your next group session to see if you have erected a wall around your heart. Think about specific people who have hurt you in the past. If you identify a wall, ask God to help you to begin tearing it down. However, realize this does not mean your heart is unprotected. You can put up a healthy, flexible boundary in its place. What steps will you take to begin tearing down the walls and restoring relationships with those you have blocked out of your heart and life?

ESTABLISHING BOUNDARIES

Identify one relationship in which you have not set clear boundaries. Write down some of the instances where you need to activate your force field. Be specific about the boundaries you need to establish. What actions will you allow and not allow? What words will you permit and not permit? At what point will you remove yourself from a situation if it becomes unhealthy?

EXTENDING COMMUNITY TO OTHERS

REFLECTIONS FROM SESSION 5

1. If you have been actively seeking to tear down a wall between you and another person, tell your group how this has impacted the relationship. How has it changed your attitude? How has it changed the way the other person sees you?
2. If you have established some clear boundaries to help you in a virus-filled relationship, what specific boundaries have you set? How has this influenced the relationship?

THE BIG PICTURE

Just a quick scan of the international scene these days reveals a level of division and murderous hatred rarely witnessed in human history. All across the world there is conflict, war, and political unrest. Sometimes I feel overwhelmed and wonder if there's any hope for a change of heart in these hotbeds of hostility. Then, every once in awhile, something deep within me whispers, "God can change the composition of human hearts. He can transform a hateful heart into a loving heart. God can bring a spirit of passionate inclusivity into hearts that have only known dispassionate exclusivity. "

And how about the national scene? An honest look at our national scene these days unmasks a level of racial resentment, division, and hostility that ought to make all of us wake up and smell the coffee. As much as we may talk about equality and all of the progress we have made to rid our nation of racism, conflicts and battles rage every day across this land.

Sometimes I look at what's going on nationally and I just sigh and wonder if there's any hope for a change of heart with regard to racial tension. But again, something deep within me whispers, "God can change the composition of human hearts."

When I look at the condition of churches around the country and around the world I am saddened as well. Sunday morning is still the most segregated time in the week. While millions of open-hearted spiritual seekers live within driving distances of churches all across our land, many churches really just don't seem to care much. There are many people just waiting to be invited, included, and enfolded into the life and community of a local church, but no one reaches out to them. Many churches today focus on peripheral matters instead of grace. Some coddle their members instead of challenging and commissioning them to open their arms and hearts to people beyond their walls. Some churches even give off subtle signals about who is welcome in their church and who isn't. Sometimes when I think about these things I just sigh and wonder if there's any hope for a change of heart in the church. Then I'm reminded yet again that God can change the composition of a human heart. God can transform apathetic hearts into strongly caring hearts. God can bring about a spirit of passionate inclusiveness into hearts that have become dispassionately exclusivistic. God can, but probably only God can.

A WIDE ANGLE VIEW

1   Where do you see a need for a dramatic change in the condition of the human heart:

- on an international level;

- on a national level;

- in your community;

- in your workplace;

- in your church?

Read Luke 15

2

The three stories recorded in Luke 15 have some
common threads running through them.

*What do they have in common, and what is the significance of
each common thread?*

3

If you had to summarize the teaching of these three
parables into one basic lesson or message, what would
it be?

Why do you feel this is the central message of these stories?

How does this message speak to followers of Christ today?

SHARPENING THE FOCUS

Read Snapshot "A Heart Exam"

A HEART EXAM

If you look at your heart closely you might discover you have a heart disease. You might find you have a case of hardening of the heart. There may be some blockage or a restricted flow of grace. In the very place where love should be coursing through your veins, you have a blockage. You might need to say, "God, is there hope for my heart? Can you touch, melt, soften and open up my heart? Can you open it up wider and enlarge its capacity to love? Can you enlarge it's capacity to extend community to a wider and wider circle of people?"

4 Take a few minutes for a time of personal reflection and prayer. Think about the questions below as you examine your own heart.

- Are there individuals or groups of people who I harbor hatred or resentment toward? If so, why do I feel this way?

- Is my heart tender and even broken over those who still don't know God's love?

- What am I doing in my life to be actively inclusive of all people in an effort to show them how much they matter to God?

Read Snapshot "Things That Matter"

THINGS THAT MATTER

In each of the three stories in Luke 15, something or someone of value ends up missing—a sheep, a coin, a son. These are not unrelated stories; there are threads that hold them together. The stories are clear that what was missing really mattered to somebody. The sheep that was missing stirred the heart of the shepherd. The coin that was lost was of great concern to the woman. The boy who wandered away mattered deeply to his father.

---

5 Tell about a time you lost something that really mattered to you.

If you eventually found it, tell about the process of searching and how you felt when you finally found the thing you had lost.

If you never found it, tell about how this made you feel.

6 How does God feel about people who are lost and don't know His love?

How does this impact the way you relate to those who are lost?

Read Snapshot "An All-Out Search"

AN ALL-OUT SEARCH

In each of the stories of Luke 15, that which was lost mattered enough to warrant an all-out search. The shepherd realizes his sheep has wandered away, so he takes off looking for it. The woman realizes a coin is missing, and she starts a search. The father in the story decides that the son needs to be in a foreign land for a while, but he longs and waits for his son's return. There tends to be a general law of life that we search for the things that matter most to us. If we lose something that holds no value to us, we don't bother searching for it. But if we lose something of great value, we commit ourselves to keep looking until we find it.

7

Who do you know that is lost and does not know the love of Jesus? Is there some way you can be an active part of the search process to bring that person home?

What can your small group members do to help in this search process?

Read Snapshot "Time to Celebrate"

TIME TO CELEBRATE

One more common thread in each of the three stories Jesus told in Luke 15 is that each of the retrievals brings rejoicing. The shepherd finds the lost sheep, brings it back, and says to his shepherd friends, "Come, celebrate with me." The woman finds the lost coin and says to her friends, "Let's celebrate." The dad has the son come home and hosts a huge celebration. In Luke 15:10 we read, "In the same way, I tell you, there is rejoicing in the presence of the angels of God over one sinner who repents."

8

How do you feel when you realize that the angels of heaven, along with the Father, the Son, and the Holy Spirit had a party on the day you became a follower of Christ?

What can you do to celebrate when a seeker friend becomes a follower of Christ?

PUTTING YOURSELF IN THE PICTURE

A MATTHEW PARTY

A Matthew party is a time when you invite your seeker friends to be with your friends who love and follow Christ. It can be a beach party, a small dinner party, a barbecue in the backyard, or any setting where you can naturally gather together your believing friends with seekers. It is modeled after the example of Matthew in Luke 5:19, when he invited all his tax-collector friends to gather for a dinner in his home with Jesus and His disciples.

Encourage your group to throw a Matthew party. Have each member of the group pray about inviting one friend who is not yet a follower of Christ. Imagine how wonderful it would be to gather with a group of growing Christ followers to mix with your seeker friends. Don't plan a big agenda, but simply create a place where you can all be together and begin building relationships.

A COMMITMENT TO CELEBRATION

In each of the three stories told by Jesus in Luke 15, there is a response of celebration. When a friend or family member becomes a follower of Christ, throw them a party, take them out for a celebration lunch, invite some folks over for an evening and rejoice with them. If anyone in your small group knows someone who has become a follower of Christ recently, plan to have some kind of celebration in their honor. Take time to join with the angels of heaven, the Trinity, and this new Christian for a time of celebration and affirmation.

LEADER'S NOTES

Leading a Bible discussion—especially for the first time—can make you feel both nervous and excited. If you are nervous, realize that you are in good company. Many biblical leaders, such as Moses, Joshua, and the apostle Paul, felt nervous and inadequate to lead others (see, for example, 1 Corinthians 2:3). Yet God's grace was sufficient for them, just as it will be for you.

Some excitement is also natural. Your leadership is a gift to the others in the group. Keep in mind, however, that other group members also share responsibility for the group. Your role is simply to stimulate discussion by asking questions and encouraging people to respond. The suggestions listed below can help you to be an effective leader.

PREPARING TO LEAD

1. Ask God to help you understand and apply the passage to your own life. Unless that happens, you will not be prepared to lead others.
2. Carefully work through each question in the study guide. Meditate and reflect on the passage as you formulate your answers.
3. Familiarize yourself with the leader's notes for each session. These will help you understand the purpose of the session and will provide valuable information about the questions in the session.
4. Pray for the various members of the group. Ask God to use these sessions to make you better disciples of Jesus Christ.
5. Before the first session, make sure each person has a study guide. Encourage them to prepare beforehand for each session.

LEADING THE SESSION

1. Begin the session on time. If people realize that the session begins on schedule, they will work harder to arrive on time.
2. At the beginning of your first time together, explain that these sessions are designed to be discussions, not lectures. Encourage everyone to participate, but realize some may be hesitant to speak during the first few sessions.

3. Don't be afraid of silence. People in the group may need time to think before responding.

4. Avoid answering your own questions. If necessary, rephrase a question until it is clearly understood. Even an eager group will quickly become passive and silent if they think the leader will do most of the talking.

5. Encourage more than one answer to each question. Ask, "What do the rest of you think?" or "Anyone else?" until several people have had a chance to respond.

6. Try to be affirming whenever possible. Let people know you appreciate their insights into the passage.

7. Never reject an answer. If it is clearly wrong, ask, "Which verse led you to that conclusion?" Or let the group handle the problem by asking them what they think about the question.

8. Avoid going off on tangents. If people wander off course, gently bring them back to the passage being considered.

9. Conclude your time together with conversational prayer. Ask God to help you apply those things that you learned in the session.

10. End on time. This will be easier if you control the pace of the discussion by not spending too much time on some questions or too little on others.

We encourage all small group leaders to use *Leading Life-Changing Small Groups* (Zondervan) by Bill Donahue while leading their group. Developed and used by Willow Creek Community Church, this guide is an excellent resource for training and equipping followers of Christ to effectively lead small groups. It includes valuable information on how to utilize fun and creative relationship-building exercises for your group; how to plan your meeting; how to share the leadership load by identifying, developing, and working with an "apprentice leader;" and how to find creative ways to do group prayer. In addition, the book includes material and tips on handling potential conflicts and difficult personalities, forming group covenants, inviting new members, improving listening skills, studying the Bible, and much more. Using *Leading Life-Changing Small Groups* will help you create a group that members love to be a part of.

Now let's discuss the different elements of this small group study guide and how to use them for the session portion of your group meeting.

THE BIG PICTURE

Each session will begin with a short story or overview of the lesson theme. This is called "The Big Picture" because it introduces the central theme of the session. You will need to read this section as a group or have group members read it on their own before discussion begins. Here are three ways you can approach this section of the small group session:

- As the group leader, read this section out loud for the whole group and then move into the questions in the next section, "A Wide Angle View." (You might read the first week, but then use the other two options below to encourage group involvement.)
- Ask a group member to volunteer to read this section for the group. This allows another group member to participate. It is best to ask someone in advance to give them time to read over the section before reading it to the group. It is also good to ask someone to volunteer, and not to assign this task. Some people do not feel comfortable reading in front of a group. After a group member has read this section out loud, move into the discussion questions.
- Allow time at the beginning of the session for each person to read this section silently. If you do this, be sure to allow enough time for everyone to finish reading so they can think about what they've read and be ready for meaningful discussion.

A WIDE ANGLE VIEW

This section includes one or more questions that move the group into a general discussion of the session topic. These questions are designed to help group members begin discussing the topic in an open and honest manner. Once the topic of the lesson has been established, move on to the Bible passage for the session.

A BIBLICAL PORTRAIT

This portion of the session includes a Scripture reading and one or more questions that help group members see how the theme of the session is rooted and based in biblical teaching. The Scripture reading can be handled just like "The Big Picture" section: You can read it for the group, have a group member read it, or allow time for silent reading. Make sure everyone has a Bible or that you have Bibles available for those who need them. Once you have read the passage, ask the question(s) in this section so that group members can dig into the truth of the Bible.

SHARPENING THE FOCUS

The majority of the discussion questions for the session are in this section. These questions are practical and help group members apply biblical teaching to their daily lives.

SNAPSHOTS

The "Snapshots" in each session help prepare group members for discussion. These anecdotes give additional insight to the topic being discussed. Each "Snapshot" should be read at a designated point in the session. This is clearly marked in the session as well as in the leader's notes. Again, follow the same format as you do with "The Big Picture" section and the "Biblical Portrait" section: Either you read the anecdote, have a group member volunteer to read, or provide time for silent reading. However you approach this section, you will find these anecdotes very helpful in triggering lively dialogue and moving discussion in a meaningful direction.

PUTTING YOURSELF IN THE PICTURE

Here's where you roll up your sleeves and put the truth into action. This portion is very practical and action-oriented. At the end of each session there will be suggestions for one or two ways group members can put what they've just learned into practice. Review the action goals at the end of each session and challenge group members to work on one or more of them in the coming week.

You will find follow-up questions for the "Putting Yourself in the Picture" section at the beginning of the next week's session. Starting with the second week, there will be time set aside at the beginning of the session to look back and talk about how you have tried to apply God's Word in your life since your last time together.

PRAYER

You will want to open and close your small group with a time of prayer. Occasionally, there will be specific direction within a session for how you can do this. Most of the time, however, you will need to decide the best place to stop and pray. You may want to pray or have a group member volunteer to begin the lesson with a prayer. Or you might want to read "The Big Picture" and discuss the "Wide Angle View" questions before opening in prayer. In some cases, it might be best to open in prayer after you have read the Bible passage. You need to decide where you feel an opening prayer best fits for your group.

When opening in prayer, think in terms of the session theme and pray for group members (including yourself) to be responsive to the truth of Scripture and the working of the Holy Spirit. If you have seekers in your group (people investigating Christianity but not yet believers) be sensitive to your expectations for group prayer. Seekers may not yet be ready to take part in group prayer.

Be sure to close your group with a time of prayer as well. One option is for you to pray for the entire group. Or you might allow time for group members to offer audible prayers that others can agree with in their hearts. Another approach would be to allow a time of silence for one-on-one prayers with God and then to close this time with a simple "Amen."

THE HEARTBEAT OF COMMUNITY

GENESIS 2:15—25

INTRODUCTION

Whenever someone makes a decision of the heart to move relentlessly toward community, that person is manifesting the stamp of a relational God. We move toward community because we were created for relationship with God and a few others with whom we can deeply connect. We will never be completely whole or fully alive until we enter into community, sincerely and fully, with God and with people. This community is the experience of knowing and being known, loving and being loved, serving and being served, celebrating and being celebrated.

Jesus, in His prayer that is recorded in the New Testament, in John 17, prayed for His disciples to find true community. He didn't pray for them to experience wealth, power, or eternal youth. No, He said, "Oh God, My Father, may they experience oneness." Relationship—deep and full communion. His desire was that they would not live in the isolation of loneliness that has never suited the souls of mankind, but would enter into community relationships that enrich, replenish, and energize their hearts and souls.

THE BIG PICTURE

Take time to read this introduction with the group. There are suggestions for how this can be done in the beginning of this leader's section.

A BIBLICAL PORTRAIT

Read Genesis 2:15–25

Question Two I was in a social setting with a young man who, by all measurements, was a rising star professionally. When I asked him how he was doing personally, he caught me off guard by saying, "Well, if you really want to know, I'm so terribly lonely that it feels like I'm dying a little bit every day." Because he knew very little about Christianity, I said to him, "You need to know that God understands what loneliness is all about, and it bothers Him more than you could ever know."

I told him that the first chapters of Genesis record God's creation of the heavens and earth. I talked to him about how God created plants and animals and, finally, the first man. I explained how God rejoiced as He finished each creative challenge by observing what He had made and saying, "It is good!" I also told him what God said after He made man: "It is *very* good!"

I then told this young man about what happened next. I recounted how God noticed loneliness developing in the soul of the first man, Adam. For the first time something in God's freshly created, spectacularly beautiful world was *not* good. God didn't go into denial, but simply called it what it was. He said, "There is something I see now that is not good—Adam's lack of community."

Adam was yearning for a deep relationship with somebody and there was no one who could meet that need. I explained to my lonely friend how God decided to spring into action and do something about Adam's loneliness. For the sake of relationship, for the sake of ending aloneness, for the sake of community, God fashioned a woman and gave her to Adam.

The woman not only addressed Adam's longing for community but, because of their reproductive capabilities, they were able to have children and therefore provide another form of community. Because God made Eve, there would be the potential of community in family and among friends, colleagues, and a wide assortment of people.

I told that young, lonely guy that deep loneliness is a condition that moved the heart of God so much that he went to extraordinary lengths to provide this wonderful concept of relationship to the human race. I explained that God wants every individual on this earth to leave the isolation and darkness of loneliness and enter into rich and lasting community.

SHARPENING THE FOCUS

Read Snapshot "Knowing and Being Known" before Question 3

Question Four Most of us can't get over the bothersome notion that if anyone knew us deeply, if anyone were to get the information about our dark side, if anyone were to ever get the key to our confidential failure file, they would probably express shock and horror and take the next stagecoach out of town, leaving us standing alone in the dust.

Even though we wish we could pour out our hearts and share ourselves with others, we lock everything up inside. We take that stuff and just push it down. We lock it up and guard the key. We still establish some friendships, but we just don't get too deep. Sometimes we spend entire evenings with people we call friends. Then we will go home, lie on the bed, and stare at the ceiling, feeling isolated and alone. We realize we relate with lots of people but nobody really knows us.

In Psalm 38 King David is longing for deep community with God. He knows he was designed and created for community with God and people. But David has a closet full of failures. He is sure that if he brings those failures out into the light they will push God away. So he keeps that information hidden, which just increases his feelings of isolation.

In Psalm 38 David cries out, "I am bent over and bowed down. I feel as though I am mourning all day long. There's no soundness in my flesh. I feel numb on the inside. I groan because of the agitation of my heart." And then he says, "my strength fails me, and the light of my eyes has gone dim." What's he saying? He saying, "I'm dying just a little bit more every day. Dying for lack of community."

Then in Psalm 51 David takes the risk of self-disclosure, and he pushes through the fear. He finally pours out all those hidden feelings and nasty secrets. Instead of abandonment; he finds in God open arms, understanding, true affection, and even forgiveness, which result in deep communion with Him. After that, David spins out psalm after psalm after psalm, expressing his astonishment at God's ability and desire to know and be known by people.

Read Snapshot "Loving and Being Loved" before Question 5

Question Six You may want your group members to finish only one of these statements instead of having each person respond to all three. This will save time and give them the freedom to pick the one that speaks the most to them.

When Jesus was asked to give the Cliff notes on Christianity, He boiled it all down to giving and receiving deep levels of love. He desires that we receive deep levels of love from God, open up our hearts to it, receive Christ, and acknowledge His gift of love for us on the cross. We are invited to return deep levels of love to Him in worship, service, and obedience. He tells us to "Love the Lord your God with all your heart and with all your soul and with all your mind" (Matt. 22:37), and to receive the love He has for us, "For God so loved the world that he gave his one and only Son, that whoever believes in him shall not perish but have eternal life" (John 3:16).

He also calls us to love people. There needs to be a deep level of loving going on with some people in and around your life. I think Jesus would say, "If you have that going on at the center of your life, you will be so enriched in your inner life that you'll probably be able to handle whatever the world and its external pressures can throw at you. You will be alive on the inside in ways you never dreamed possible."

Whereas fear often immobilizes us when it comes to knowing and being known, I think, among other things, ineptitude often restrains us from loving and being loved. I think most of us feel loving toward a number of people, but many of us lack the skills necessary to convert feelings of love into appropriate expressions that communicate it powerfully and convincingly to others.

Read Snapshot "Serving and Being Served" before Question 7

Questions Seven & Eight Some time ago I met with a guy who had gone through life without feeling a real need for the help of others. He'd been a success without them. But then a life-threatening disease had swept over his body and he had to go into a surgery from which he might not return. A few months after his surgery I sat in his office with him. He was a different man. He said, "My family and my friends put wash-cloths on my forehead and bent the straw so that I could drink ice water. They bathed me. They took care of things at the house. They sent me cards and letters. They served me." The experience transformed his understanding of relationships. It happened because of serving and being served. For the first time the man began to discover the wonder of community.

That's what serving does. It warms up fires. It keeps the whole concept of relational dynamics going. So if you have a relationship that's getting a little cold, if you have a friendship that's a little bit stuck, if you want to move a little closer to the kind of community or oneness that Jesus prayed for His followers to experience in John 17, then I would challenge you to think of a way you can help carry someone else's burden. Think of a way you could lift someone's spirits or perform just a small act of kindness. Think of a way you could serve somebody or be open as someone tries to serve you. Don't be stronger than you need to be. Don't be more independent than you need to be. Learn to serve and learn to allow others to serve you and watch the community blossom.

Read Snapshot "Celebrating and Being Celebrated" before Question 9

Question Nine I was with a small group of guys many years ago on a sailing trip. We were sitting in the cockpit of a sailboat after dinner one night. It was dark, and we were staring at the sky. I said, "Let's finish this sentence for each other as a gift. If you were suddenly taken out of my life, I would miss your ___."

One guy said to another guy, "If you were taken suddenly out of my life, I would miss your joy, your laughter, your exuberance. You breathe so much life into me. If you were taken out of my life, I don't know what I would do."

Then someone else said, "If you were taken out of my life, I would miss your leadership and your wisdom, your insight and your guidance."

Someone else said, "If you were taken out of my life, I would miss your love for God and your spiritual enthusiasm."

We went around the group, and we finished that night in genuine community. It was rich, and it was alive. We all need to learn that we can do that for each other. We can celebrate each other. We can celebrate and be celebrated.

PUTTING YOURSELF IN THE PICTURE

Let the group members know you will be providing time at the beginning of the next session for them to discuss how they have put their faith into action. Let them tell about how they have acted on one of the two options above. However, don't limit their interaction to these two options. They may have put themselves into the picture in some other way as a result of your study. Allow for honest and open communication.

Also, be clear that there will not be any kind of a "test" or forced reporting. All you are going to do is allow time for people to volunteer to talk about how they have applied what they learned in the previous session. Some group members will feel pressured if they think you are going to make everyone report on how they acted on these action goals. You don't want anyone to skip the next group because they are afraid of having to say they did not follow up on what they learned from the prior session. The key is to provide a place for honest communication without creating pressure or fear of being embarrassed.

Every session from this point on will open with a look back at the "Putting Yourself in the Picture" section of the previous session.

COUNTING THE COST OF COMMUNITY

PHILIPPIANS 2:1—4

INTRODUCTION

When God wired us up, He created us with a desire to know and to be known, to love and to be loved, to serve and be served, to celebrate and be celebrated. We were created to be in rich relationship with God and others. We were created for community. However, most of us have discovered that building deep friendships and lasting community takes a lot of hard work and energy. If we are going to have lasting, meaningful relationships, we need to be ready to pay the price and invest in the lives of others.

Proverbs 17:17 says, "A friend loves at all times, and a brother is born for adversity." The Bible teaches us that friendship is one of the richest experiences we can have in life. We're born for relationships. They makes our hearts bigger and keep us steady in a storm. Relationships help end our aloneness. However, we need to give of ourselves and work at developing deep friendships and community with others.

THE BIG PICTURE

Take time to read this introduction with the group. There are suggestions for how this can be done in the beginning of this leader's section.

A WIDE ANGLE VIEW

Question One Allow your group members to give simple and basic definitions of each term. These are words we often use but may not be able to define as easily as we might think. It might be helpful to look back at the last session for some helpful definitions for what is valuable and important in our relationships.

I once listened to an economist give a lecture about the national indebtedness. There was a question and answer session following his presentation. Economic theories were flying around the room so fast it would make your head spin. Finally, things seemed to get so jumbled up that people were asking questions that didn't make any sense. The economist said, "Well, maybe we'd better go back to the basics." He said, "We need to understand the difference between spending and earning. When you spend money, money goes *away* from you. When you earn money, money comes *toward* you." Then he said, "You need to have more money coming toward you than you have going away from you if you're ever going to balance a budget." This simple illustration reminded me of the importance of clarifying basic definitions.

A BIBLICAL PORTRAIT

Read Philippians 2:1–11

Question Three Philippians 2 gets right at the core of a radical idea. It says, "You want to know what's really at the heart of friendship? It's determining to seek the interest of the other person." This is a totally countercultural idea. We are invited to seek the interest of our friends above our own desires. It's about leaving the shadows of hiddenness to take parts of your heart and entrust them to the care of others. It's the joyful surrender of your own agenda once in awhile for the sheer pleasure of meeting a need or bringing a smile to the face of a friend. It's the consistent resistance of the urge to be independent, self-centered, manipulative, superficial, or narcissistic. It's agreeing with God's internal pattern that urges you to open up your heart to live in loving community with others.

Jesus not only called us to engage in these kinds of relationships, He set the standard. Jesus took risks, gave of Himself, served others, and invested in the lives of a small group of people. He left the glory of heaven and perfect community with the Father for the sake of entering relationship with us.

SHARPENING THE FOCUS

Read Snapshot "Friendship Is Not" before Question 4

Questions Four & Five If you're going to move into community, you need to start by making sure you have the right idea about the nature of friendship. It might be helpful to clarify what friendship is *not*, before we look at what it is.

Friendship is not trying to get someone to take care of you. Do you want to wreck the possibility of a relationship? Go into it with the idea that there's someone out there just sitting on a park bench waiting to nurture you, soothe you, comfort you, and listen endlessly to your troubles and travails. Do you want to wreck the possibility of a relationship? Go in expecting that the other person is just hungering to affirm and encourage you.

If that's the expectation you're bringing into friendship, it's not a good one. The fact is, when your potential friends discover your idea of friendship, they'll make themselves curiously scarce and you'll continue to be alone. Fundamentally, friendship is not trying to get someone to take care of you.

Friendship is also not hitching your life to a rising star so that you can progress professionally, academically, financially, or politically. I have spent some time in Washington, D.C., and I am sometimes made aware of how shamelessly people use and discard others in that city for self-advancement purposes. This is often done under the guise of friendship.

Friendship is not pretending to care about someone so that they'll join your cause, buy your product, sell your product, or attend your church. You just can't build friendships of integrity with wrong motivations.

Real friendship involves the genuine exchanging of knowledge, kindness, service, and celebration. It's a growing commitment among peers to seek the well-being of each other. In our world, that's a radical concept.

Read Snapshot "Friendships Take Work" before Question 6

Question Six Sometimes when you're mining for gold and you think you've found it, you get all excited until you find out it's fool's gold. Then you're let down and hurt. But you keep excavating and you keep trying. That's a lot like building a friendship. There is a price to be paid up front for the eventual discovery of the thing we call community. We would all prefer a drive-up window style of building friendships and community. We would love to custom order just what we want in a relationship and be sure we can "Have it our way!"

However, friendship-building is not that easy. Seldom do we find a relationship that's premade, premixed, and free of awkwardness and error along the way. There are no shortcuts to body-building, knowledge-building, faith-building or relationship-building. They all require the development of an internal desire that's strong enough to push through the false starts and stops that are bound to happen in the friendship-development process.

When it comes to finding lasting friendships, you might just have to excavate. But when you get a nugget of that stuff—when you get a piece of relational gold—you'll say it was all worth it. You can't put a dollar value on real friendships and deep community. They're priceless.

Read Snapshot "Friendships Take Time" before Question 7

Question Seven Most of the time there is that uneasy, awkward phase of friendship development when we first meet someone. We don't know if it's possible to build a friendship, but we are curious and willing to try. We dabble in some surface-level conversations and subconsciously wonder if there might be the makings of a friendship there? We begin to invest some time into the life of the other person with the hope that a friendship will develop.

Because this phase of friendship-building is so awkward, uncomfortable, and potentially hurt-filled, lots of people dabble in it once or twice, and if it doesn't work, they bail out. They go home night after night in order to avoid the potential hurt of trying to build friendships. They yearn for community but never find it, because they've taken themselves off the playing field. They are not willing to invest the time it takes to build deep relationships.

Other people try it once or twice, and if it doesn't work out they get bitter at the world. They say, "I don't like my neighborhood; the people are not friendly." Or they complain, "The church I attend is not friendly at all." It's my experience that most people are friendly. The real question is, "Am I willing to put my heart out there and try to build friendships, even if it takes energy and time?"

The problem is rarely the neighborhood we live in, the church we attend, or where we work. It's usually me. It's you. We have to work at developing relationships and community. We have to count the cost, invest the time, and be willing to live with a few bruises and bumps along the way. The question is, "Are you willing to count the cost of building friendships?"

Putting Yourself in the Picture

Challenge group members to take time in the coming week to use part or all of this application section as an opportunity for continued growth.

MOVING BEYOND SUPERFICIALITY

JOHN 4:4—26

INTRODUCTION

We live in a superficial world. In our microwave culture, we too often settle for relationships that stay on the surface. We don't take the time to dig deeply into community and learn how to move beyond the barrier of superficiality into the rich soil of relationships. This session focuses on how we can move into deeper levels of relating to others.

Not only do we need to count the cost of moving into community with each other, but we also need to discover those things that will help nurture deeper levels of communication and relationship. We need to press beyond our comfort zone and learn to ask questions that will open the door to rich conversations. In this session we will work on developing our ability to ask questions that break the superficiality barrier. Also, we will discover the essential need for a vital and deep relationship with God if we are going to have meaningful relationships with others.

THE BIG PICTURE

Take time to read this introduction with the group. There are suggestions for how this can be done in the beginning of this leader's section.

A BIBLICAL PORTRAIT

Read John 4:4–26

Question Two Most of us want to move into deeper patterns of relating with others. However, in many cases, we don't know how to break the barrier of superficiality and move to a deeper level of communication. In this passage we read a story about deep communication from the life of Jesus.

Jesus is on a trip with His twelve disciples. At midday He stops at a well to rest for a little while. The disciples go into town to buy food, and while they are gone, a Samaritan woman comes to the well to draw water. In those days the Jews had nothing to do with the Samaritans. And Jewish men did not relate with women in public settings. Yet when this Samaritan woman came to draw water, Jesus took the initiative and said, "Would you please draw me some water to drink?"

Now here's how the conversation *could have gone*. It could have just been very shallow and superficial.

Jesus could have said, "Good water."

And the woman could have said, "Good well."

And then Jesus could have said, "Very wet, refreshing."

And the woman could have said, "It's a hot day, don't you think?"

Jesus could have said, "Yes, very hot. Thanks for the drink. . . . Have a nice day."

Jesus and the woman could have stayed right there on the surface—the place most of our conversations remain. But look what happened. The woman took a risk. She went up to Jesus and said, "How is it that you, being a Jew, would treat me, a Samaritan woman, like a human being? I'm curious. What's going on in your mind and heart that you would make such a dramatic break with social convention and treat me with dignity?"

That woman took a relational risk. She broke beyond the superficiality barrier. By posing one simple question, she opened the door to a conversation that eventually came around to personal, spiritual, moral, and eternal issues. The conversation that followed changed the whole course of her life.

SHARPENING THE FOCUS

Read Snapshot "Moving Beyond Superficiality" before Question 3

Questions Three & Four There are many things that can keep us relating on a surface level rather than moving to deeper levels of community. Many people live with unexpressed fear of intimacy. They desire to move deeper in relationships, but at the same time, they are terrified at the idea of opening up themselves to others. Fear keeps many people from breaking the superficiality barrier.

For others, the problem may be that they have bad communication patterns. They have never made any effort to go deeper in conversation and develop community with others. Their parents were not very expressive, and all they have ever seen are examples of poor communication. They have not watched others risk, dig deep, or work through issues. Instead, they have learned from unhealthy examples and are now simply repeating the history of their parents.

There are also people who have tried to move deeper in relationship but have been burned. They have opened their heart, taken risks, and have been treated badly. Because of the scars they have from past experiences, these people have decided they will no longer risk getting hurt again.

If you have a fear of opening your life to others, if you have never seen good examples of deep communication, if you have been burned in the past, or if something else stands in the way, I challenge you to be willing to try again. Deep relationships and friendships are worth their weight in gold. Although they take work and can be hard to develop, you must never stop seeking to build strong and lasting community.

Read Snapshot "The Value of a Good Question" before Question 5

Question Five "What question do we ask almost everybody whenever we see them?"

It's, "How are you doing?" The standard answers, of course, are: "Fine, good, fair, not bad." To which we respond, "All right, see ya."

When you discern that it is an appropriate time and place, you will be amazed at what people will tell you if you ask this question just a little differently. Simply say, "How are you doing, *really*?"

Tell your friend, "I have a few moments and would love to listen to whatever you would like to talk about. How are you doing, really? How are things at work, really? How are things at home, really? How are things at church, really?"

There's another question I use that has taken half my life to figure out. When someone tells me about something that is happening in their life, I say, "How do you feel about that?"

A friend says, "I broke up with my girlfriend."

A surface response might be: "Did you get all your CDs back?"

A better question would be, "Well, how do you feel about that?"

Another question I use a lot, especially with my kids, is, "What are you thinking right now?"

I was in the car with my son Todd one day. He was sixteen years old at the time. He was really quiet for a while. Finally I said, "Todd, what are you thinking about right now?"

He gave me the standard, "Oh, Dad."

I said, "You know, Todd, I just want you to know that what-ever you're thinking about right now, I'm interested in it. If it's your car, kids at school, sailing, anything, it doesn't matter. I like to know what you're thinking about because I love you; your thoughts are important to me."

A few minutes later he said, "Well, I was thinking about. . ." and he started a conversation.

When we were done talking I said, "Thanks for talking to me about what you were thinking. Thanks for trusting me with your thoughts."

Read Snapshot "The Place of Community with God" before Question 6

Question Eight We all wish there was someone who would be there for us—all the time. We wish someone was concerned about our well-being. We wish we were the center of some-one's world. We wish we were the object of someone's full affection. These desires are part of the way God has wired us.

The problem comes when we try to get these needs met from other human beings. We put stress on friendships that others can't bear. Then we get our nose out of joint and feel hurt because others don't meet our high expectations. With time, we raise our expectations higher and higher and pretty soon people are saying, "I've got to stay away from this person. If I let them down, it seems to destroy them." Instead of drawing people toward us, these high expectations drive them away.

God says, "Look, here's the deal. I have love of another kind. I have an uncontaminated, focused, high-octane affection for you. I have love that will flow like a white-water rapids out of my heart into the hearts of those who will open up to Me. My love is consistent and pure. You are the object of My full affec-tion. You are the center of My world. You are what I think about twenty-four hours a day. You are precious to Me. I gave My Son to die on the cross so that you could come into full relationship with Me." When we understand how much God loves us, we are in a much better place when it comes to giving and receiving love in human relationships.

PUTTING YOURSELF IN THE PICTURE

Challenge group members to take time in the coming week to use part or all of this application section as an opportunity for continued growth.

HEALING RELATIONAL VIRUSES

ROMANS 12:9—13

INTRODUCTION

We live in an imperfect world filled with imperfect people. The truth of the matter is, there is no such thing as a perfectly healthy relationship between two human beings. There are all kinds of relational viruses floating around, and we are bound to catch some of them as we seek to live in community with others.

In this session we will seek to honestly identify some of the relational viruses that infect our lives. To do this, we must be honest and willing to examine our own family background, relational history, and the condition of our heart. If we do this prayerfully and consistently, we will see some wonderful healing in our relationships and lives.

THE BIG PICTURE

Take time to read this introduction with the group. There are suggestions for how this can be done in the beginning of this section.

A BIBLICAL PORTRAIT

Read Romans 12:9–13

Question Three This discussion could take the entire time you have designated for your small group. Rather than have everyone try to respond to each area of challenge, invite group members to identify one of the challenges that speaks to them. Encourage practical examples of how following this word of encouragement could help build a strong and healthy relationship. You might also want to ask how a relationship might be impacted if this quality was taken away.

Sharpening the Focus

Read Snapshot "Meeting the Smiths" before Question 4

Question Four Relationships aren't working well anymore. They're exceedingly more complicated than they were thirty years ago. There are more relationship viruses out there, so healthy relationships are harder and harder to build. An acquaintance of mine recently filed for divorce, which shocked everybody around him. When he was asked why he did it, he simply lowered his head and said, "Three months after I married this woman, I found out how deeply angry she was at the way her father had treated her when she was growing up. She's been a rage-filled woman for twenty years, and even though I've pleaded with her to get help to work through the anger, she'd never do it. Twenty years of duty with a venom-filled woman is all I can bear." This woman had a virus she did not want to see or deal with.

Another woman I know is dying on the inside just a little bit every day because her over-achieving husband can't stand not setting a new sales record every year at work. The woman just wants to be noticed, appreciated, touched, and nurtured, but it doesn't look hopeful. It takes eighty hours a week for her husband to keep his top sales position. He's got a virus that could cost him more than he might ever imagine.

Another very capable professional woman I know just got a pink slip at work because her performance intimidated her insecure male boss. He's got a virus. Relationship-building is a lot more complicated today than it's ever been before. We all need to learn how to identify the viruses infecting our relationships and do all we can to get rid of them.

Question Five Many relational viruses can be remedied with some reading on the topic, attending a seminar, dialoging with other relationally mature people, praying, or developing some disciplines or accountability points. Admittedly, some viruses are far more complex and may require a few trips to a friendly Christian counselor's office for the healing process to begin. Other viruses are so deep they might take an extended time of counseling and a great deal of prayer and spiritual support from friends. But you must know you will never reach your relational potential in your marriage, with your kids, or with your friends, until you identify and deal with these viruses.

We all have viruses in our relationships, but many of us also have stories of how God has brought healing in our relational life. Being honest about our struggles, as well as telling each other about our victories and growth, can help in the healing process.

Question Six I know a guy who shrinks back from every new activity and opportunity because he grew up in a home where his self-esteem and self-confidence were undermined daily. He brings a fear virus to his relationships. When he starts building a friendship and someone accepts him, he winds up clinging too tightly because he's afraid they might abandon him if he lets go. His fear ends up driving others away—the very thing he fears most. He needs to face his fear and get support as he develops healthy relationships.

Do you know what your virus is? Do you have the humility to realize that you have one or more? Do you realize what it's doing to your friendships and family relationships? It's time to face the reality that we all have viruses that can destroy our relationships. It's also time to get support from other followers of Christ as we seek to build health in our relationships.

Read Snapshot "Examining Your Relational Health" before Question 7

Putting Yourself in the Picture

Challenge group members to take time in the coming week to use part or all of this application section as an opportunity for continued growth.

SETTING HEALTHY RELATIONAL BOUNDARIES

EXODUS 18:13—27

INTRODUCTION

In a world filled with relational viruses, we will catch every virus that comes around unless we have boundaries in our relationships. In other words, without boundaries, relationships can be very unhealthy.

The goal of this session is to challenge group members to they live with no boundaries or with a wall around their heart. Either extreme is unhealthy. We need to create flexible boundaries that leave us open to love and be loved while protecting ourselves from those who have severe relational viruses and who can damage our hearts and lives.

THE BIG PICTURE

Take time to read this introduction with the group. There are suggestions for how this can be done in the beginning of this section.

A BIBLICAL PORTRAIT

Read Exodus 18:13–27

Question Three Moses needed a person who was older and wiser to come to him and challenge him to establish some relational boundaries. He was letting everyone come and dump the cares of their lives into his lap. He still needed to love the people and help them; however, he did not need to do everything himself. He needed help. He needed support. There were times he needed to say, "I can't meet your needs." He needed to have boundaries.

SHARPENING THE FOCUS

Read Snapshot "Living Without Boundaries" before Question 4

Question Five It might be helpful to pause as a group and pray for those people who have expressed some of the pain they have experienced because they have not lived with clear relational boundaries.

Read Snapshot "Unhealthy Walls" before Question 6

Question Seven Your minister may be teaching from the Scriptures, telling you things you need to know, talking about the love of Christ, teaching about the realities of heaven and hell. But you're an expert at functioning behind walls. While that minister is speaking truth from the Word of God, you're saying, "I don't buy any of it. He's an egomaniac who's trying to draw a crowd to himself. He's not going to affect my heart." This kind of "protection" and cynicism can be deadly. If this is the condition of your heart, it's time to tear down some walls.

Many men are fantastic wall builders. They learn how to do the masonry and get their walls airtight. That's why many women say, "I just cannot attain a sense of intimacy with my husband. We just don't connect." Most men know the temptation to be a wall builder. They learned from the time they were a boy not to get hurt—that they could overcome any obstacle if they just toughed it out. Men are told to compete, win, and build those walls to keep everything in order. They don't get hurt much, but they often lead lonely lives.

Read Snapshot "Flexible Boundaries" before Question 8

Question Eight Jesus condoned celebrations and joyous festivities. He went to wedding celebrations and loved attending parties so he could be with people. However, there were some people in those days who came to Jesus and falsely accused him of being a glutton and a wino. They made sure everyone knew how they felt. But note, we don't read that Jesus went and cried all night because he was mortally wounded by those accusations. Neither do we read that he got angry and looked for a chance to get back at them.

Jesus knew their accusations were unfounded. He had enough presence of mind and relational skill to erect boundaries. It was as if Jesus said, "You can make every false accusations you want to—that's your problem. I know what I did. It was appropriate. It was well within the will and the parameters of God, My Father. I know I am in good standing with Him.

While you listen to a pastor preach, you have the ability to activate your boundaries. If the pastor is teaching on some area you've got under control and the Holy Spirit has given you a sense of affirmation about it, you can activate that force field and say, "Other people might need work on this. I'm doing fine."

Other times the pastor may be preaching and the Word of God is coming straight at you. You say to yourself, "This is just for me." Then you lower the force field. You drop those boundaries down and say, "Oh God, speak to me through this. I need to hear it. I need to learn about it. I need to act on it. It's for me." Then you keep the boundaries down.

When "Cousin Eddie" comes over asking for a handout, you say, "Eddie, sit on the other side of the table. We're going to talk before I get out my checkbook. I've given you loans five times, Eddie. What happened to them? Let's be honest. What do you really need here? Money, or help with some deeper issues? If you can build a good case, I'll lower my boundary. I'll write you the check; I'll do it with joy. But if you're conning me, Eddie, then I'm going to erect this force field. I'm not going to write you the check, and I'm not going to feel guilty about it."

Boundaries give us the ability to have discernment and to protect ourselves from being hurt over and over again. We need to learn when to have them up and when to have them down if we are going to live with healthy relationships.

PUTTING YOURSELF IN THE PICTURE

Challenge group members to take time in the coming week to use part or all of this application section as an opportunity for continued growth.

EXTENDING COMMUNITY TO OTHERS

LUKE 15

INTRODUCTION

How's your heart today? I wonder what's going on inside of it. I wonder how open your heart is to people. How open is your heart to people of ethnic diversity or a different color? How open is your heart to people of higher or lower educational status than you. How open is your heart to people who are higher or lower on the socio-economic ladder? How open is your heart to people who differ from you politically? How open is your heart to people who are far from God and who give every indication they're not likely to reconsider their spiritual waywardness anytime soon?

Too often we become exclusive in our attitudes. We push away the very people we should be caring for and loving. This session is a challenge to be more inclusive of others. God wants us to know that He loves those people who are lost. He wants us to adopt His tender heart toward them. Lost people matter to God, and they warrant an all-out search. We need to do all we can to reach them. And when they finally are found and come home, we need to celebrate!

THE BIG PICTURE

Take time to read this introduction with the group. There are suggestions for how this can be done in the beginning of this leader's section of your small group study guide.

A BIBLICAL PORTRAIT

Read Luke 15

Question Two The Pharisees were bothered watching Jesus conversing with crowds of irreligious seekers. Many of these religious leaders wished the earth would open up and swallow these irreligious scoundrels who couldn't get their spiritual act together.

Jesus knew their hearts were cold toward these folks so He turned to the Pharisees and said, "I'm going to tell you three stories." This is the only time in the entire teaching ministry of Jesus that He uses three parables—back to back to back. I believe Jesus is saying, "I am going on record in this moment to settle in your minds, once and for all, about who matters. So I'm not going to risk telling you just one or two stories. Here we go—back to back to back—I'm going to rapid-fire truth into you so you'll get it once and for all!"

Jesus said to the Pharisees, "Here are my three stories—a lost sheep, a lost coin, and a lost son." The stories are painfully simple if you just look at them on a surface level. A shepherd has a hundred sheep, one wanders off, he searches for it until he finds it, brings it back, and calls his shepherd friends together to rejoice with him. A woman has ten coins, loses one, searches the house, finds it, and celebrates with her friends. A dad has two boys. The younger demands his inheritance, takes off, blows it recklessly in a foreign land, and returns home begging to be a hired hand who lives in the bunkhouse. But the father warmly embraces the son, forgives him, and throws a party on his behalf.

They may seem a little unrelated on the surface, but there are threads that run through these three stories. If you can identify the hidden truths of these three stories, and if you allow these truths to sink deeply into your soul, your heart will change. Your arms will open wider. You will be a more loving, inclusive person.

The common threads I see in these stories are: 1) Something of great value is lost; 2) There is a time of seeking or searching; and 3) There is celebration when that which was lost is finally found. The message of these parables is about lost people. They really do matter to God, and they should matter to us. They should matter so much that we take part in the search process and celebrate when they are finally found.

Question Three One day Jesus was surrounded by a crowd of spiritual castaways. These were the kind of people who make most upstanding church folks bristle, the kind whose morals, values, and vocabulary were not acceptable. The crowd was listening to Jesus with riveted attention. While Jesus was talking, the religious leaders of that day, the scribes and the Pharisees, took note of Jesus' interaction with "those kinds of people" and began murmuring among themselves. They felt that someone of Jesus' stature should be more careful about the company He kept. He should show more discernment than to associate with those kinds of folks.

Surely, these religious leaders reasoned to themselves, any thinking person knows that there are some people who should be included and some who ought to be excluded. There are some people who need to be shown the entrance to places—and some who need to be shown the exit. There are some people who should sit in the front of the bus and some who should sit in the back. There are those with accents and there are normal people who speak like us. There are people who vote on the wrong side of every political issue and people who get it right every time. There are movers and shakers and there are deadbeats. The Pharisees had it all figured out. They knew which people in their society had value and which people didn't. They knew who mattered and who didn't matter at all. And it bothered them that Jesus was so undiscerning as to waste His time with the undesirable kinds of people.

Before we judge the Pharisees too harshly, it is my long-held belief that every human being carries in his or her heart an unpublished but quite conscious list of who has value in this world and who does not. It is a part of our shadow side. It's a reflection of our fallenness, the manifestation of evil at work within us. We need to examine our own hearts and identify prejudice or hatred for others. Before we go judging the Pharisees, we need to ask ourselves, "Are there people who I tend to exclude or avoid?" If so, we need to pray for a change of heart and a deeper love for all people. They matter to God, and they should matter to us.

Sharpening the Focus

Read Snapshot "A Heart Exam" before Question 4

Question Four I've been with folks before—and so have you, I'm sure—who have conveyed a disgust bordering on outright hatred for certain ethnic groups or races or entire countries. What are they saying? What does this demonstrate?

I'm ashamed to admit it, but in unguarded moments, when I least expect it, my heart turns cold and hard toward certain kinds of people. I find myself freezing them out, keeping them away, setting them aside, excluding them. In those moments, it breaks my heart to realize that I don't want to know and be known by them, I don't want to love and be loved by them, I don't want to serve and be served by them, and I don't want to celebrate and be celebrated by them.

It is an all-out tragedy that the very people who matter to God can be ignored and excluded by those of us who already follow Christ. Remember that list I talked about? Part of growing as a spiritual person is becoming more aware of our list and looking for ways to erase it. The further we move up the road of spiritual development, the shorter our list becomes. Our goal should be to have no list at all!

Read Snapshot "Things That Matter" before Question 5

Question Six I remember windsurfing with my son when he was about six years old. I know now, by hindsight, that it was unwise to do this, but I used to take Todd out on Lake Michigan in the big waves on a windsurfer. I'd put a little lifebelt around his waist and throw him up on my shoulders. He would squeal with delight and yell, "Jump the waves, Dad, go faster!" One day we were out about three-quarters of a mile from shore when I saw a squall blowing in. I said to Todd, "Hey, Todd, this has to be our last run because there's a storm coming in and we'd better get back to the beach before it hits us." He said, "Aw, Dad, we're going so fast—let's just make one more run." I said, "Oh, all right." So we made one more run and ended up way out from the shore when the squall hit us. I couldn't hold the power of the wind in the sail. The waves were getting bigger and bigger. I hit a wave and the wind overpowered the sail. We were catapulted in different directions off the windsurfer. When I finally came up from underneath the water, the waves were so big that when I was on top of a wave looking around for my son, I couldn't see him. When he was on top of a wave, I'd be in a trough. I really thought I'd lost him. So I started screaming. I screamed so loud that I pulled all my vocal cords and some of my chest muscles. I screamed at the top of my lungs, "Todd! Todd! Todd!"

Then by the grace of God, at one point both of us were on top of a wave and I saw his little blond head. I started kicking and swimming toward him as fast as I could. When I grabbed hold of that little boy I just held on tight and thought, *I'll never let this kid out of my arms again.* In those moments when something or someone precious is missing, the only thing that matters in the universe is for you to get them back.

Do you know what Jesus was saying to the Pharisees when he told the stories of a lost sheep, coin, and son? He was saying, "These spiritual scoundrels that I'm hanging out with—these lost people—their condition stirs my heart so much that there's nothing else in the universe that matters as much as getting them back. I want them in my family where they belong. I long to see them born again, forgiven, cleansed, and brought into community with God the Father." Jesus was saying to these Pharisees, "Don't write them off! Don't harden your heart! Don't close up and become exclusivistic. Don't do it! Because if you knew how much these folks mattered to the Father and how much they matter to me, you'd never have a cold heart toward them again."

The reality of that truth ought to melt the hardness of our hearts. When you realize how God feels about people, you start saying to yourself, "I guess I've never met eyes with someone who doesn't matter to God." Then you start realizing that every person you interact with today, tomorrow, the next day, and every day the rest of your life is someone who matters to God—a man, woman, or child for whom Christ died. Pretty soon you start thinking, *People ought to matter more to me. My heart should be bigger toward them. My arms should open wider. I should be passionately inclusive of every breathing, walking human being.*

Read Snapshot "An All-Out Search" before Question 7

Read Snapshot "Time to Celebrate" before Question 8

Question Eight In all three stories in Luke 15, retrievals brought rejoicing. At the end of this teaching, Jesus lets us know that there is a party in heaven every time a person becomes a follower of Christ—a vast party all across heaven with all the saints, angels, and the Trinity there. And over the head table is a banner with the name of the one who was lost but has been found.

I grew up in a home where we did not have lots of parties or celebrations. It's hard to describe what happened in my heart when I realized that all of heaven rejoiced when I repented and came to faith. I have a vision in my mind of this cosmic celebration that took place in heaven in my late teenage years when I repented and asked Jesus Christ to be my Savior. There was a banner over the head table. And MY NAME was on that banner! I remember thinking, "I can't believe I matter that much."

If you've trusted Christ, there was a time when you repented and gave your life to Christ and all of heaven exploded in a cosmic celebration. There was a banner with your name on it! Heaven celebrated because you matter so much and you were finally brought into community—into the fold. You were no longer lost—you were found.

PUTTING YOURSELF IN THE PICTURE

Challenge group members to take time in the coming week to use part or all of this application section as an opportunity for continued growth.

ADDITIONAL WILLOW CREEK RESOURCES

Small Group Resources

Coaching Life-Changing Small Group Leaders, by Bill Donahue and Greg Bowman
The Complete Book of Questions, by Garry Poole
The Connecting Church, by Randy Frazee
Leading Life-Changing Small Groups, by Bill Donahue and the Willow Creek Team
The Seven Deadly Sins of Small Group Ministry, by Bill Donahue and Russ Robinson
Walking the Small Group Tightrope, by Bill Donahue and Russ Robinson

Evangelism Resources

Becoming a Contagious Christian (book), by Bill Hybels and Mark Mittelberg
The Case for a Creator, by Lee Strobel
The Case for Christ, by Lee Strobel
The Case for Faith, by Lee Strobel
Seeker Small Groups, by Garry Poole
The Three Habits of Highly Contagious Christians, by Garry Poole

Spiritual Gifts and Ministry

Network Revised (training course), by Bruce Bugbee and Don Cousins
The Volunteer Revolution, by Bill Hybels
What You Do Best in the Body of Christ—Revised, by Bruce Bugbee

Marriage and Parenting

Fit to Be Tied, by Bill and Lynne Hybels
Surviving a Spiritual Mismatch in Marriage, by Lee and Leslie Strobel

Ministry Resources

An Hour on Sunday, by Nancy Beach
Building a Church of Small Groups, by Bill Donahue and Russ Robinson
The Heart of the Artist, by Rory Noland
Making Your Children's Ministry the Best Hour of Every Kid's Week, by Sue Miller and
    David Staal
Thriving as an Artist in the Church, by Rory Noland

Curriculum

An Ordinary Day with Jesus, by John Ortberg and Ruth Haley Barton
Becoming a Contagious Christian (kit), by Mark Mittelberg, Lee Strobel, and Bill Hybels
Good Sense Budget Course, by Dick Towner, John Tofilon, and the Willow Creek Team
If You Want to Walk on Water, You've Got to Get Out of the Boat, by John Ortberg with
    Stephen and Amanda Sorenson
The Life You've Always Wanted, by John Ortberg with Stephen and Amanda Sorenson
The Old Testament Challenge, by John Ortberg with Kevin and Sherry Harney, Mindy
    Caliguire, and Judson Poling

WILLOW
Willow Creek Association

Willow Creek Association
Vision, Training, Resources for Prevailing Churches

This resource was created to serve you and to help you build a local church that prevails. It is just one of many ministry tools that are part of the Willow Creek Resources® line, published by the Willow Creek Association together with Zondervan.

The Willow Creek Association (WCA) was created in 1992 to serve a rapidly growing number of churches from across the denominational spectrum that are committed to helping unchurched people become fully devoted followers of Christ. Membership in the WCA now numbers over 12,000 Member Churches worldwide from more than ninety denominations.

The Willow Creek Association links like-minded Christian leaders with each other and with strategic vision, training, and resources in order to help them build prevailing churches designed to reach their redemptive potential. Here are some of the ways the WCA does that.

- **The Leadership Summit**—a once a year, two-and-a-half-day conference to envision and equip Christians with leadership gifts and responsibilities. Presented live at Willow Creek as well as via satellite broadcast to over 130 locations across North America, this event is designed to increase the leadership effectiveness of pastors, ministry staff, volunteer church leaders, and Christians in the marketplace.

- **Ministry-Specific Conferences**—throughout each year the WCA hosts a variety of conferences and training events—both at Willow Creek's main campus and offsite, across the U.S., and around the world—targeting church leaders and volunteers in ministry-specific areas such as: small groups, preaching and teaching, the arts, children, students, volunteers, stewardship, etc.

- **Willow Creek Resources**®—provides churches with trusted and field-tested ministry resources in such areas as leadership, evangelism, spiritual formation, spiritual gifts, small groups, stewardship, student ministry, children's ministry, the use of the arts—drama, media, contemporary music—and more.

- **WCA Member Benefits**—includes substantial discounts to WCA training events, a 20 percent discount on all Willow Creek Resources®, *Defining Moments* monthly audio journal for leaders, quarterly *Willow* magazine, access to a Members-Only section on WillowNet, monthly communications, and more. Member Churches also receive special discounts and premier services through WCA's growing number of ministry partners—Select Service Providers—and save an average of $500 annually depending on the level of engagement.

For specific information about WCA conferences, resources, membership, and other ministry services contact:

Willow Creek Association
P.O. Box 3188
Barrington, IL 60011-3188
Phone: 847-570-9812
Fax: 847-765-5046
www.willowcreek.com

What You Do Best in the Body of Christ

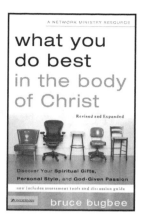

Discover Your Spiritual Gifts, Personal Style, and God-Given Passion

Bruce L. Bugbee

Have you found fulfillment in life? Can you say your ministry is fruitful? God has created you to be both fulfilled and fruitful in a meaningful place of service. You can discover your God-given design and the role he created for you in and through the local church.

In *What You Do Best in the Body of Christ*, Bruce Bugbee helps you identify your God-given spiritual gifts, personal style, and ministry passion. And he shows how they point to your unique role and purpose in the body of Christ when they are expressed together. Drawing from biblical principles, this book provides proven tools and a conversational approach that will help you fulfill God's will for your life. You'll discover:

- Your God-given Spiritual Gifts indicate what you're equipped to do competently
- Your God-given Personal Style indicates how you can serve with energy and authenticity
- Your God-given Ministry Passion indicates where you're motivated to serve

Together, they indicate what you do best in the body of Christ!

You will also better understand God's design for the church and your role within it.

You'll find plenty of helpful charts and self-assessments—plus insights into the fallacies and pitfalls that can hinder your effectiveness. Start learning today what God wants you to do, and experience more enthusiasm, greater joy, and real significance in your life and ministry.

Softcover: 978-0-310-25735-6

Pick up a copy today at your favorite bookstore!

ZONDERVAN®
.com

WILLOW
Willow Creek Resources

Discover Your Spiritual Gifts the Network Way

Bruce L. Bugbee

This is a small booklet containing five assessments in the areas of traits, observations, experiences, convictions, and ministry fit to help people understand their spiritual giftedness. This tool offers a totally unique resource for identifying a person's spiritual gifts through several perspectives or approaches. People who take a one-dimensional assessment often wonder how accurate it really is. When they are able to take multiple assessments indicating some common conclusions, it increases their confidence and motivation to serve accordingly. This tool has the opportunity to set a new standard for gifts-identification, just as Network has with the Servant Profile (passion, gifts, style) identification, consultation, and placement process.

Softcover: 978-0-310-25746-2

Pick up a copy today at your favorite bookstore!

ZONDERVAN®
.com

WILLOW
Willow Creek Resources

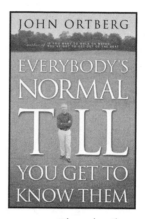

Leading Life-Changing Small Groups

Bill Donahue and the Willow Creek Small Group Team

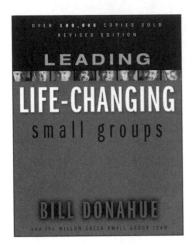

Like nothing else, small groups have the power to change lives. They're the ideal route to discipleship, a place where the rubber of biblical truth meets the road of human relations.

As director of adult education and training at Willow Creek Community Church, Bill Donahue knows that small groups are key to building biblical community and thriving individuals. In *Leading Life-Changing Small Groups*, Donahue and his team share in-depth the practical insights that have made Willow Creek's small group ministry so incredibly effective.

The unique, ready-reference format of *Leading Life-Changing Small Groups* gives small group leaders, pastors, church leaders, educators, and counselors a commanding grasp of:

Group formation and values
Meeting preparation and participation
Leadership requirements and responsibilities
Discipleship within the group
The philosophy and structure of small groups
Leadership training
And much more.

From an individual group to an entire small group ministry, *Leading Life-Changing Small Groups* gives you the comprehensive guidance you need to cultivate life-changing small groups . . . and growing, fruitful believers.

Softcover: 978-0-310-24750-0

*Look for Leading Life-Changing Small Groups
at your local Christian bookstore.*

Pick up a copy today at your favorite bookstore!

Walking the Small Group Tightrope

Bill Donahue and Russ Robinson

Leading a successful small group is like walking a tightrope. You traverse a taut, exciting line, balancing the dynamic tensions characteristic of every group. Drawing from the concept of "polarity management," Bill Donahue and Russ Robinson help you understand and deal with six dynamic areas every group leader must manage in order to create genuine, transforming small group community.

Your group is in for unprecedented connection and growth when you harness the interplay between Truth and Life; Care and Discipleship; Friendship and Accountability; Kindness and Confrontation; Task and People; and Openness and Intimacy.

Effective, life-giving small groups learn how to embrace both ends of each continuum. *Walking the Small Group Tightrope* will strengthen your sense of balance, help you gain confidence as a leader, and show you how to release the untapped creative and relational energy in your group.

Softcover: 978-0-310-25229-0

Pick up a copy today at your favorite bookstore!

Continue building your new community!

New Community Series

Bill Hybels and John Ortberg
with Kevin and Sherry Harney

Exodus: Journey Toward God 978-0-310-22771-7

Parables: Imagine Life God's Way 978-0-310-22881-3

Sermon on the Mount1: Connect with God 978-0-310-22884-4

Sermon on the Mount2: Connect with Others 978-0-310-22883-7

Acts: Build Community 978-0-310-22770-0

Romans: Find Freedom 978-0-310-22765-6

Philippians: Run the Race 978-0-310-23314-5

Colossians: Discover the New You 978-0-310-22769-4

James: Live Wisely 978-0-310-22767-0

1 Peter: Stand Strong 978-0-310-22773-1

1 John: Love Each Other 978-0-310-22768-7

Revelation: Experience God's Power 978-0-310-22882-0

Look for New Community at your local Christian bookstore.

Continue the Transformation

Pursuing Spiritual Transformation

John Ortberg, Laurie Pederson,
and Judson Poling

Grace: An Invitation to a Way of Life 978-0-310-22074-9

Growth: Training vs. Trying 978-0-310-22075-6

Groups: The Life-Giving Power of Community 978-0-310-22076-3

Gifts: The Joy of Serving God 978-0-310-22077-0

Giving: Unlocking the Heart of Good Stewardship 978-0-310-22078-7

Fully Devoted: Living Each Day in Jesus' Name 978-0-310-22073-2

Look for Pursuing Spiritual Transformation at your local Christian bookstore.

Tough Questions
Garry Poole and Judson Poling

Softcover

Reality Check Series
by Mark Ashton

Share Your Thoughts

With the Author: Your comments will be forwarded to the author when you send them to *zauthor@zondervan.com*.

With Zondervan: Submit your review of this book by writing to *zreview@zondervan.com*.

Free Online Resources at
www.zondervan.com/hello

 Zondervan AuthorTracker: Be notified whenever your favorite authors publish new books, go on tour, or post an update about what's happening in their lives.

 Daily Bible Verses and Devotions: Enrich your life with daily Bible verses or devotions that help you start every morning focused on God.

 Free Email Publications: Sign up for newsletters on fiction, Christian living, church ministry, parenting, and more.

 Zondervan Bible Search: Find and compare Bible passages in a variety of translations at www.zondervanbiblesearch.com.

 Other Benefits: Register yourself to receive online benefits like coupons and special offers, or to participate in research.

ZONDERVAN®
.com